TOGETHER
for
HARVEST

a resource anthology

CHURCH INFORMATION OFFICE
Church House, Dean's Yard, Westminster, SW1P 3NZ

ISBN 0 7151 0345 8

Published 1976 for the General Synod Board of Education

Reprinted 1982

© Central Board of Finance of the Church of England, 1976

Printed in England by Bocardo & Church Army Press Ltd., Oxford

CONTENTS

FOREWORD

For the teacher, harvest is one of the most exciting and creative festivals of the year—in spite of the fact that it has no official place in the modern Church Calendar. It can be explored in so many aspects: the wonder, beauty and variety of God's creation; the reliability of the natural laws which fulfil his promise ' Seedtime and harvest shall not fail '; the age-old thankfulness for the gifts of bread and wine, which to a Christian mean a deeper reason for gratitude; Man's responsibility towards the created world and also towards his hungry neighbours who are equally the heirs of creation. . . . The list is endless and so is the cry for new approaches, new ways of enabling the old to be seen as fresh, relevant, significant.

We have tried to meet this need by asking some of our most popular contributors to *Together* for new, *unpublished* material. With one or two exceptions, the services, stories, hymns and topics in this book have not previously appeared in the magazine —unlike the items in our two previous anthologies, *Together for Christmas* and *Together for Festivals*. So even if you are a regular subscriber (as we hope), you won't have seen these ideas before!

Please don't forget that they are only ideas—suggestions upon which to build. Don't feel that they must be copied word for word. If you feel, ' We could do something better with that idea,' then take the plunge, go ahead and do it. It will be better, because it will be yours and your children's. This is really important—you, not this book, are the best resource you have.

And may you have a happy, creative and memorable harvest festival. . . .

Pamela Egan
Editor, *Together*

HARVEST FESTIVAL— WHAT'S THE POINT?

Alan Beck looks at the reasons for the popularity of services at harvest time, and suggests how those who come from nostalgia can be helped to true worship

There are those who are rather sniffy about Harvest Festival because it isn't in the Church Calendar, whereas Lammas is. They have a point, for Lammas has much to teach us, celebrating as it does the making of the first loaf from the new corn, and bringing this as an offering to God. It is the Church's original harvest festival, and encouraged man to respond in gratitude as soon as God's mercies were shown, not when all is safely gathered in and we know if it has been a good harvest or a poor one.

But few people now bake their own bread, let alone grow their own corn and mill their own flour. Bread is no longer the main item in our diet, and indeed bread—white, sliced and wrapped—is not what it used to be, so perhaps it is not surprising that Lammas has faded away. What is surprising is the way Harvest Festival has caught on. Its invention in the nineteenth century coincided with the removal of the majority of the population of this country from personal contact with the land, yet it is as popular in town and city parisdes as in the country.

Is it religious nostalgia? A sentimental harking back to a (never-existent) rustic paradise? It is easy to be cynical in the face of so much in English people's attitude to religion that is only nostalgia: the picture of the little old village church with the sheaves of corn (now virtually unobtainable) propped up in the porch. It is about as true to life as the Christmas card depicting the stage-coach in the snow as the epitome of Christmas—when in fact it was a slow, cold and extremely uncomfortable mode of transport and nothing to do with Christ's incarnation whatsoever! But if people do come out of nostalgia, we must ensure that having come, we take them much deeper, for Harvest Festival can express two fundamental aspects of religion—the goodness of God, and Man's need to respond.

Gratitude is the obvious message of harvest. We can draw this out by starting with some home-produced crop and considering all those involved in producing it, agricultural workers, rail and road transport, market, shop, parent who bought it, prepared it, served it, and the breadwinner who earned the money to pay for it. We can then take some imported object, e.g. a banana, to show how we depend on the labours of people in distant lands, and dock workers, sailors, sometimes airline pilots and workers. The simple objects in any church at harvest can take us round the world and into almost any industry you can think of, e.g. packets and cans take us into the paper and steel industries. Gratitude for the work of others carries with it the message of world-wide mutual responsibility and interdependence. We are immediately into the realm of social conditions and wages in the food-producing countries.

From this we can go on to gratitude for the good earth in which the crops grow, and for seas and rivers, and thus into conservation and the theological truth that the earth is the Lord's and not man's to exhaust, overcrop and overfish. We are into stewardship in its widest sense. We can go still further into the mystery of life itself contained in every seed.

Secondly comes 'response'. There is within us a deep instinct and need to give to God something that we have produced and which has cost us a good deal in care and pains. Particularly is this needed for those whose daily work consists of a monotonous repetition of some tiny task on a mass-production line. People who have little creative satisfaction at work often make up for it in their leisure time in their garden or allotment. One may laugh at the outsize marrow but it can be an expression of this fundamental religious instinct to make a sacrifice to God. We find this instinct in all religions and it occupies an important place in our Old Testament. It is a great pity that so few penetrate beyond the aspects which are offputting to our modern squeamish susceptibilities, for sacrifice was and is a joyful thing and lies at the heart of true worship.

One way of avoiding unreality in Harvest Festival is to consider 'harvest' in the widest sense. A true local harvest may be the product of local industry. Some are too bulky to bring into church—an atomic power station, for example! But when such a new station began generating for the first time and feeding into the National Grid, a local parish which included many of the power station construction engineers could thank God for a

3

harvest of atomic power which was at that moment lighting the church and providing power for the organ. North Sea oil and gas are two new harvests and the direct connection between fuel and food is now becoming widely appreciated—fuel for tractors, for oil-based fertilisers, etc. Other local harvests may be more homely things like shoes, or clothes, or even babies. For parishes with large new housing estates, this may well be their true harvest.

Looked at like this, Harvest Festival need never become stale and repetitive, for the possibilities are endless, and if we succeed in leading people to genuine gratitude and grateful giving, then we have taken them to the heart of true religion.

CELEBRATING MICHAELMAS

Alice Goodman suggests ways of looking anew at a festival with roots deep in our countryside

The end of September is the time for Harvest Festivals, and we are generally so preoccupied with this in our day and Sunday schools that most of us never give Michaelmas Day a thought.

Yet the Festival of Michaelmas was once a great occasion, and one of the Red Letter days in the Church's year. Here are some suggestions for a new look at a very ancient festival.

Most of us hardly ever think about angels, and indeed, there is not a great deal that we know about them. Yet we have no reason to doubt that they exist. Angels are a natural and believable part of the Christmas Story to children. Gabriel's appearance to Mary, the multitude of the Heavenly Host praising God after announcing to the shepherds the news of a Saviour's birth . . . we cannot think of Christmas or sing many Christmas carols without a reminder of them.

Here it is worth thinking of other occasions in the New Testament when angels are mentioned. We read they helped Jesus at the Temptation and the Agony in the Garden of Gethsemane. Two were at his tomb when the stone was found rolled away, proclaiming the glad news. An angel freed Peter from prison and was near St Paul on board ship. The word ' angel ' just means ' messenger ' and the early Church believed that God used his particularly special messengers when it was necessary that there should be no mistake about the news they had to carry. Angels are an expression of our belief in God's active care for his world and, indeed, his whole universe. St Michael, in St John's vision, is seen as the chief of the angels, and the Early Church regarded him as the chief of the Archangels, one of whom was Gabriel, who are at constant war with the Devil on our behalf. Thus, Michael is the patron saint of soldiers, and the Jews also looked to him as the protector of their Temple in Jerusalem.

The Christian Church in early days, similarly hoped Michael would be the guardian of the Church. In the Middle Ages, therefore, Michaelmas Day was a great Feast Day. A holiday (holy-day) was allowed, and on this day, great Michaelmas Fairs were held. Some of these were sponsored by large abbeys and churches, and they generally did very well out of this arrangement. People came together at fairs in the Middle Ages to trade, and to enjoy themselves, and Michaelmas was a particularly important Fair in addition because it was generally a Hiring Fair also.

Farm labourers were engaged from one Michaelmas to the next. By the end of September, the main Harvest had been gathered, and so the year on the farm was considered at an end. Rows of labourers stood waiting to be hired at Michaelmas Fairs. Each wore a token of his trade: the shepherd a tuft of sheep's wool in his hat, the carter a piece of whip-cord, the cow-man a tuft of cow-hair, while the maids carried a mop. As soon as the man or woman had obtained a situation, the token was removed and exchanged for a ribbon bought with the token penny given to seal the bargain: this was called a fairing.

Children can make strips of figures by paper-folding, dress them in smocks, etc., with cut paper, and give them various tokens to be worn at a Michaelmas Hiring Fair.

After the end of September the winter rain and snow could be expected fairly shortly, so the poor roads rapidly became quite impassable in many places, and everybody settled down for a long winter. Michaelmas was therefore a ' last fling ' before winter, and the next festival would not be until Christmas.

Goose was a traditional dinner for Michaelmas Day, and Goose Fairs were common at that time. The geese might have to walk long distances to market, wearing, it is said, ' shoes ' made from sand and tar to protect their feet. This is now a thing of the past, and the old Goose Fairs at Michaelmas are held merely for ' all the fun of the fair ' today.

A group picture can be made of a Michaelmas Goose fair, using a few stencils if the children are too young to draw their own. Large numbers of geese can be used, some being driven along the road, some in pens at the fair. Old records mention as many as twenty thousand geese having been driven along the roads to one such fair!

Michaelmas was also a ' Quarter Day '. By paper-folding, or on a chart on the wall, the children can mark all the old ' Quarter Days '.

They were: Lady Day, March 25th.
Midsummer Day, June 24th.
Michaelmas Day, September 29th.
Christmas Day, December 25th.

Each of these quarters can have appropriate decorations on the chart. Daffodils, roses, Michaelmas daisies and holly are obvious examples. But the children should realize that Michaelmas was the most important of the four in the country economy of olden times. Farm rents, cottage leases and work engagements began and ended at that time.

None of us needs reminding how to make simple decorative angels as part of the classroom display at Christmas. Our window-sills are always full of them, and they swing from ceilings and walls.

Try making them on the feast of St Michael and All Angels. You will have more time then to think about the role of angels with the children. As we say at the Communion Service,

'Therefore with Angels and Archangels. . . .'.

NO APPLES?

A story to be danced, drawn or mimed—Ivy Russell recounts the true tale of Johnny Appleseed

People don't have to be great heroes or heroines in order to help other people. Sometimes the very simplest deeds are the ones that are remembered longest.

John Chapman was born in America in the year 1801. It was a time when pioneers were making perilous journeys across the continent to open up new settlements, and when John was old enough he went off adventuring, too.

Life was hard in those days, and pioneers had to carry all their own equipment and cooking utensils. It would have been foolish to carry anything that wasn't really necessary, so instead of taking a hat, John wore a saucepan on his head. It kept off the sun, and it was ready to use when he needed it for cooking.

One thing that John discovered when he reached the part of America which we now know as Ohio, was that there were no apple-trees there. Now this was a pity, because the poor people who were struggling to make a living there would have been glad of a crop of apples. So he had an idea.

He made his way back east again, to the more civilised region of Pennsylvania where he knew there were cider presses; and there he collected a sack full of apple seeds. Then, slowly and with difficulty, travelling sometimes on horseback and sometimes by canoe, he journeyed back to Ohio again.

Sometimes on the way he would meet with Indians, but John loved all his fellow men, and would greet them with a smile and a gift of beads or food. So he arrived safely in Ohio, and there he made camp near a fair-sized settlement. He cleared a patch of ground, and in it he planted his seeds. He watched over them carefully till they grew into saplings big enough to transplant, and then he gave them around to the pioneers.

He did this many times over the years that followed, until gradually the state of Ohio became bright with the blossom of

8

apple-trees. And when Harvest-time came, the hard-working farmers were able to gather ripe apples to help feed their families.

It is hard for us to realise what a wonderful gift these were, for we have shops near at hand where we can buy all the food we need. But the early settlers were hundreds of miles from shops, and they must have thanked God with all their hearts for the kindness of the man who is known to this day as Johnny Appleseed.

JETHRO TULL:

Man of ideas

Sarah Parkes introduces someone who could spark off an investigation of agricultural pioneers, or provide the basis for an address at school or family service

For hundreds and hundreds of years seed was sown by the same method: the sower carried the seed in his pouch and scattered it in handfuls on the ground. Much of it was wasted; eaten by birds or falling on rocky soil or among the weeds. Changes in farming came very slowly.

Over three hundred years ago Jethro Tull was born—in 1674. He was an innovator—a man with new ideas. He thought of new ways of sowing seed so that from the least seed the biggest crop would grow. By observation and experiment he discovered that it was more economical to use only the best seed and to sow it thinly and carefully. He saw that it grew best if sown thinly and in neat rows, so that the soil between the rocks could be tilled frequently to keep the weeds away.

His farmworkers refused to sow as he suggested. No doubt they said: 'It's too bothersome; it's too new; new ideas are bad ideas.'

So Jethro Tull thought that a machine might do the work that the men refused to do. He invented a drill that would sow the seed sparingly and in neat rows. It was some time before his ideas were understood.

But other men were also working to improve farming: to grow better corn for bread; to breed healthier cattle and sheep and so more milk and meat and wool. Their work, in time, meant that the poor would not be so cold and hungry. Today, all over the world, men and women are working to ensure food for everyone.

In England, where the soil is good, we need two square yards of farmland to make a loaf.

In much of the world they need seven square yards of land to make a loaf. Yet bread is so badly needed; as indeed, is food of all kinds.

Most of all people need to know how to grow their food better; they need men and women with ideas like Jethro Tull, truly an innovator; and they need water, drainage and tractors, all the things that go to make good farming.

There is a proverb that says:

Give a man a fish and you feed him for a day.
Teach him how to fish and you feed him for a lifetime.

We could also say:

A loaf will feed a family for a day.
Seed well sown will feed them for a lifetime.

'THANK YOU'

A theme for 3s to 6s
by Gill Bick

The aim of our work was to explore all aspects of thankfulness and to discover the happiness of being ourselves and accepted by God in his family just as we are.

As we worked through each section, any pictures the children did were kept until the end, to form a book for each child which had, stuck to its front cover, a note explaining the aim to parents.

To begin with, the children were encouraged to talk about and draw their favourite presents. We talked about giving as well as getting and we began to learn the chorus ' Thank you, thank you, Jesus ' (from *Sounds of Living Water*, published by Hodder & Stoughton).

In the next phase the children brought pictures of beautiful things, and we talked about being able to see. We played simple games like ' Blind Man's Buff ' and guessing by feel objects hidden in socks. The children were able to look at a Braille version of ' Peter Rabbit ', feel the tiny dots, and to write ' thank you ' in Braille.

We then moved on to sound and hearing, with favourite records and songs. We made shakers out of plastic bottles to use when singing the ' Thank you ' chorus.

After this we began talking about what makes us happy. The children were asked to find out what made their parents happy—and we got some interesting answers! We had a funny story about a man with a large house, 32 beds—and no friends, because he hadn't learnt to say thank you or please. Together we found we were happiest when doing things with others, usually (at this age) with Mum and Dad or brothers and sisters. Even the three-year-old who said that what made him happy was ' dinner ', sat down to it with his family. We began to see the importance of our families, and we talked about God's family as well.

During our final session the children all drew pictures of themselves and we stuck these on the cover of their book, with the words ' Thank you, God, for making me—me! ' This is the

12

chorus of the Butterfly Song (*Sounds of Living Water*) which the children had also learnt to sing.

All their work was stapled into book form and we displayed these books in the church at Family Service, to be taken home afterwards. During the service the children sang the two songs and used the decorated shakers, not as a performance laid on for the parents but as an expression of joy and thankfulness for all God's goodness to us and for what we were learning together. Our service in fact included a baptism, but our theme could be tied in just as satisfactorily with Harvest, for it gets over the point of thankfulness not only for material things, but for the fact that God will love and accept us just as we are.

CRAFTS FROM COLLECTIONS

Alice Goodman has ideas for using Nature's autumn bounty in the classroom

Nature offers an extravagant hand-out of collectable material at Harvest-time, and most children are great collectors. From the fallen leaves they will select the most colourful, their pockets will be filled with conkers and acorns, masses of hips and haws will be brought to school—often an embarrassment of riches to a classroom with limited space for display.

The question, often unspoken, is 'How can I use all this?' Here are a few suggestions in which children's own skill and inventive effort can provide them with an answer. Generally, they only need to be started off!

1. Collages

The use of seeds and fruits to make an attractive collage is not a new idea, but the decisions on subject matter are all too often made by the teacher. If a few varied examples are shown first, children enjoy planning their own. This makes a useful group or individual activity or competition.

2. Collecting Fruits of Plants

Too many town children think of fruits as the edible variety in the greengrocer's shop only. It is a new idea to them that every plant produces a fruit of some kind containing a seed or seeds. Starting from the fruits of trees which are not edible, it is useful to show children some of these different plant fruits, and let them make a collection. So many seeds are scattered in autumn that this certainly is not an activity which robs the countryside.

The collection, when made, can be classified by the children in various ways. For example, there are the juicy fruits and berries, the dry fruits which split to release the seeds, the fruits with sticky or 'burred' cases for animal dispersal, and so on. Another method of classification is to sort the fruits into sections according to where they were found, e.g. fruits of trees, of the hedgerow, of plants found in woods, meadows or waste land.

14

I once was walking round the display tents at an autumn agricultural show, when I saw on view collections made by children on the lines I have described. Their ingenuity was remarkable; many entrants had made display trays divided by card or match-box trays into small sections. Each contained a labelled fruit of some plant or tree. A collection like this can provide a useful and educative holiday occupation.

Reference books will be needed from a school or public library in order to identify some of the specimens. A leaf of each plant, or a flower, if any are left, should also be included with the fruit. This is a help to the teacher when she checks that the specimens have been correctly named.

3. Leaf Printing

In spring, the leaves of trees are too soft to be of much use for this purpose. By the autumn however, when leaves are ready to fall, the veins are firm and hard. The undersides of the leaves, if covered with stiffish paint, or with shoe blacking (have a care here!) and then pressed onto white paper, give clear prints. These can be used in decorative ways, or as reminders of tree identification by the different leaves.

Generally, a little practice is required first, before the children are ready to work on ' best ' paper.

4. Model-Making using Natural Materials

Some children have the imagination, skill and patience to use natural materials in model-making, and this medium has an attraction all its own. You have only to recall the use of it at St Paul's Cathedral, where the Crib and Nativity Scene were constructed solely of natural materials, to grasp what possibilities there are.

A simple start can be made by encouraging children to examine natural materials, some of unusual shape, and compare their likeness to animal and other forms. In the early stages, of course, the children will need to use match-sticks, card and so on as embellishments. Later, they find it a challenge to endeavour to dispense with these aids.

All kinds of natural materials can be used, of which there are a profusion in autumn at Harvest-time. These include straw, sticks and logs of various sizes, autumn fruits, dried grasses, and so on. The secret is to be constantly on the watch, and children are helped in their observation by this means.

The ancient custom of making corn dollies and their use is interesting, and though the sight of beautifully made and intricate corn dollies is a bit daunting to the teacher who may not be artistically gifted, it is still possible for children to make simple ones. These can be made in the way most of us can remember making woolly golliwogs, when we were children. Simply fold over about a dozen strands of pliable straw in half, tie at the 'neck' with raffia or string, insert a similar but shorter bundle across for 'arms' and secure with ties at wrists and waist. The legs are made by dividing the straw and tying each half at the 'foot' end.

Having made the corn dollies, explain to your children how ancient is the story of wheat-growing. Because this was discovered, men stopped roaming about in search of food, and settled down to live in communities. They also discovered that wheat and other grains could be stored and eaten in the winter, and when planted in the spring would yield a fresh supply.

It was hardly surprising, faced with this stupendous discovery, that early peoples believed that corn had divine power. To cut and harvest it was therefore, in a sense, like killing or insulting the god of the corn. Ceremonies were held at Harvest, when the forgiveness of the corn gods was sought, and we think corn dollies might have been part of the rites.

SING A SONG OF HARVEST

Written by Alan Davies for a school harvest service, this can be sung to a tune of your choice or spoken by single and grouped voices

1. Sing a song of harvest,
   Sing a song of wheat.
   The grain is in the barn,
   There'll be enough for all to eat.
   The tractors have stopped
     chugging,
   The combines put away,
   So sing and shout for joy there
   On this thanksgiving day.

2. Sing a song of fishermen,
   The North sea trawling fleet
   Fighting with the weather
   With waves at thirty feet.
   So pull upon the nets, lads,
   If you want to last the day,
   And sing and shout for joy
     there
   On this thanksgiving day.

3. Sing a song of vegetables,
   Sing of beans and marrows,
   The ones that are so heavy
   That you wheel them round in
     barrows.
   Sing a song of brown eggs
   Lying in their trays,
   So sing and shout for joy there
   On this thanksgiving day.

4. Sing a song of overseas
   And all the harvest there,
   People of all colours
   Who come from everywhere.
   Sing a song of harvesters
   From lands across the way,
   So sing and shout for joy there
   On this thanksgiving day.

5. Sing a song of miners
   Who work beneath the ground
   Sing a song of oil and coal
   And everything they found.
   Sing a song of planes and ships
   To send us on our way,
   So sing and shout for joy there
   On this thanksgiving day.

6. Sing a song of poverty, *(slowly)*
   Sing a song of greed,
   Sing a song of hunger,
   Sing a song of need.
   Sing a song of starving
   And falling by the way,
   Without a song or shout of joy
   On this thanksgiving day.

7. The harvest is all safely in
                        (slowly)
   So why make such a fuss?
   It's no use to the starving
   If the harvest's all for us!
   So think before you sing for joy,
   So think my friends, and pray
   For those who have no harvest
   On this thanksgiving day.

8. Sing a song of harvest,
   Sing a song of love,
   Sing a song of sun and rain
   That comes down from above.
   Sing a song of helpfulness
   And care so that we may
   Sing and shout for joy here
   On this thanksgiving day.

9. Sing a song of sharing,
   That no-one goes without.
   That is what the harvest
   Is really all about.
   Shout for joy to God, then,
   As we go on our way,
   Just sing and shout to God here
   On this Thanksgiving day.

TREES IN AUTUMN

This poem by Alan Davies was written to accompany a series of slides taken in the grounds of his Solihull school, and was taped with suitable music. Its theme of new life is complementary to that of harvest

The autumn leaves stand clear against the sky
As if to lay warm golden fingers on the cold clear depths of space
And give one final blessing to the passing summer, gentle as a sigh.
Those golden coins of autumn
Spilling out from nature's precious till,
None wasted, none forgotten, none ignored,
But all invested in the promise of a springtime yet to come.
The golden magic carpet still 'tween heaven and earth
Will soon take wing, and then come floating down
Each one a piece of nature's precious tapestry,
And each unique, never to be again.
Drifting and swirling they will come to rest
On road and field, pavement and garden lawn,
Chasing each other, tossed by impish winds
Or blown in drifts like piles of golden snow.
Then see them frolic in a whirl of glee,
Searching in spirals for the branch from whence they came
As if remembering their golden days:
But golden days are over for a while
And one by one the leaves say their farewells
In bonfire smoke, or compost piles,
Or nestle back into the earth which gave them birth . . .
And they are gone . . . but only for a while,
For from their hidden resting place
They push fresh life, and whisper, ' Spring is here! '
And nature eager for her cue, will burst out fresh and green.
The pageant of the trees begins again,
And somewhere life will always start anew.

WHO CARES?

by Ivy Russell

Now all is safely gathered in,
The church is like a bower
With golden corn and harvest loaf,
With scent of fruit and flower.

Our hearts are full of gratitude,
For it is good to know
There is enough for all our needs
Come wind or frost or snow.

But far away across the sea
A farmer views his land,
A wilderness of withered stalks,
In earth as dry as sand.

Too sick at heart to kneel and pray,
His cry sounds piteously,
' My children die for want of food.
Who cares for such as we? '

Lord, all is safely gathered in;
Now show us how to share
These precious fruits of harvest with
Your children everywhere.

'GOD ALMIGHTY SET A RAINBOW'

This hymn by Caroline Somerville can be sung to 'Z-Cars' or 'My darling Clementine', or to more formal tunes like 'Austria', and 'Zum Frieden'.

God Almighty set a rainbow
Arching in the sky above,
And his people understand it
As a signal of his love.

Chorus: Thank you, Father, thank you, Father,
Thank you, Father, for your care,
For your warm and loving kindness
To your children everywhere.

Clouds will gather, storms come streaming
On the darkened earth below—
Too much sunshine makes a desert,
Without rain, no seed can grow.
Thank you, Father . . . .

Through the stormcloud shines your rainbow
Through the dark earth springs the wheat;
In the future waits your harvest
And the food for men to eat.
Thank you, Father . . . .

God Almighty, you have promised
After rain the sun will show;
Bless the seeds and bless the harvest.
Give us grace to help us grow.
Thank you, Father . . . .

THE BYFIELD HARVEST HYMN

How this hymn came to be written by Phyllis Taylor

The children were rehearsing their Harvest Festival hymn, ' Fair waved the golden corn '.

> ' And full of joy each shining morn
> Went forth the reaper band. . . .'

' What were they going to do ? ' asked the teacher.
' They were going to play a tune,' said one seven-year-old.
' My Dad plays in a band too.'

It was this incident that led Phyllis Taylor—who was the teacher concerned—to write the harvest hymn which you will find opposite. She says, ' Those of us whose memories go back to the beginning of the century find the Victorian hymns evocative of the harvest fields with their ranks of golden sheaves, but it did not dawn on me until this happened that they rouse no appropriate response in the child of today, whose experience is of the magical achievements of the combine harvester.

' But on Harvest Festival Sunday our church looks so beautiful that I longed for a hymn in which the children could feel themselves involved and which would recall to them, when they are my age, memories of their own childhood.'

The Rector of Miss Taylor's church in Byfield, Northampton, the Rev. Andrew Bowden, adds, ' Many of the old favourite hymns use pictures of a country life which has long since disappeared. The harvest festival is just as important an event as ever it was, with produce from gardens and allotments displayed in the church. What we need are the new hymns which will express the new situation, and Miss Taylor's seems to do just that.'

The hymn, with music by the then headmaster of the village school, Mr Cameron Fraser, was first sung at a united harvest service for Anglicans and Free Church members.

THE BYFIELD HARVEST HYMN

Let young and old with merry noise
together tell the story
that ends again in harvest joys
and autumn's golden glory.
For man has worked all day in field,
in garden spent his leisure,
that earth her choicest fruits may yield
to crown the year with pleasure.

Now hips and haws of scarlet hue
the morning sunshine dapples,—
tomatoes and cucumbers, too,
and grapes, and pears and apples.
Within the church the feast is spread
on window-sills and ledges,
with home-made loaves of farm-house bread,
and berries from the hedges.

The young ones bring their gifts today
with grateful hearts and voices,
and thus that loving care display
in which our Lord rejoices.
Potatoes, carrots, peas and beans,
and clumps of purple daisies,
with marrows, beetroot, sprouts and greens
They offer, singing praises.

Mothers and sisters have their share—
adorning church and chapel;
preserving damson, plum and pear
and chutney, rich with apple.
Now ears of wheat are full and sweet
and bread is on the table,
and we will all, in church and hall,
sing loud as we are able;—

' Thank you, O God, for blessings given
and, most for that Communion
which lifts our hearts to highest heaven
when we with you have union.'
So once again with merry noise
we all tell forth the story
that ends each year in harvest joys
and autumn's golden glory.

© Phyllis Taylor. Tune © Cameron Fraser

A THANKSGIVING FOR FARMERS

by F. Pratt-Green with a simple tune by Stanley Fuller

JONGENS ♩=80

When loaves are on the table,
  Who sees a field of wheat?
Or thinks about the farmer
  Who grew the food we eat?

Perhaps in bitter weather
  He had to plough and sow,
As gulls behind the tractor
  Reminded him of snow.

And while the seeds were hidden
  Beneath the frozen earth,
He had to trust to nature
  To mother them at birth.

He watched for those diseases
  That harm the tender grain,
And feared to see his acres
  Lie rotting in the rain.

But there's a joy of harvest
  That everyone may know:
The happiness of reaping
  The best that we can grow.

When food is on the table,
  And there is bread to eat,
Thank God for every farmer
  Who has a field of wheat!

Tune © Stanley Fuller

Words of this and the following carol by permission of Oxford University Press.

THE FESTIVAL OF THE FIRST-FRUITS

by F. Pratt-Green based on Deuteronomy 26. 1–15

CHERRY TREE CAROL

Traditional English Carol Melody

Come, sing a song of harvest,
    Of thanks for daily food!
To offer God the first-fruits
    Is old as gratitude!

Long, long ago, the reapers,
    Before they kept the feast,
Put first-fruits in a basket,
    And took it to the priest.

Shall we, sometimes forgetful
    Of where creation starts,
With science in our pockets
    Lose wonder from our hearts?

May God, the great Creator,
    To whom all life belongs,
Accept these gifts we offer,
    Our service and our songs;

And lest the world go hungry
    While we ourselves are fed,
Make each of us more ready
    To share our daily bread.

HARVEST SONG

Words and music by Pamela Verrall©

1. We thank you Lord for all the food that Har-vest brings us now, And we will still re-mem-ber the hand that guides the plough. For fro-zen foods we're grate-ful. For canned or bott-led too But we will still re-mem-ber the coun-try where they grew.

2. We thank you, Lord, for fisher-folk
And for the food they bring,
For cod and plaice and herring,
With thankful hearts we sing.
For lobsters, crabs and crayfish,
For pearly oysters too.
But we will still remember
The stormy seas and you.

3. We thank you, Lord, for all the warmth
Around us ev'ry day.
We thank you for the riggers
And oil-wells far away.
For miners too, we thank you,
For coal of blackest hue.
But we will still remember
The dangers, Lord, and you!

27

BABY SWALLOW LEARNS A LESSON

by Ivy Russell

Mrs Swallow had four babies; and although three of them were quite ordinary little birds who did nothing but eat and sleep and cry for food, Teeny-weeny was very different. He was always looking and listening and asking questions.

Their nest was just under the roof of a house, and not far below was a window. There was nothing Teeny-weeny liked better than listening to what the Man of the house had to say.

'Oh, mummy!' Teeny-weeny cheeped one day. 'The Man is so clever. He says he built this house all by himself!'

'Did he indeed?' twittered Mrs Swallow. 'I happen to know that he had three men to help him, and all kinds of machinery. Now, we swallows build our own houses too, but we have nothing to help us except our beak and our wings.'

Teeny-weeny thought about this for a long time, while he ate and slept and grew a bit bigger.

'Oh, mummy!' he cheeped, a few weeks later. 'The Man really is clever. Today he went to the river and caught a big fish for his dinner.'

'Did he indeed?' twittered Mrs Swallow. 'Well, we swallows catch our own dinner every day—and some for our babies as well. And we have nothing to help us but our beak and our wings.'

Teeny-weeny thought about this for a long time, while he grew bigger and bigger, and learned to flutter around the house.

'Oh, mummy!' he cheeped one day in early autumn. 'Do you know what the Man is going to do next? He's going to fly to Spain for a holiday in a great big aeroplane. Isn't he clever!'

'Come and sit on this telegraph wire with me, Teeny-weeny,' said his mother. 'I see it is time you and I had a little talk.'

Then Mrs Swallow and her children went and sat on the wire, and all their friends gathered round to listen.

'Every year,' said Mrs Swallow, 'for as long as anyone can remember, we swallows have flown to Spain for our winter holiday. Sometimes we go even farther, to Africa. And we don't have aeroplanes to carry us—just our two little wings. Now, Teeny-weeny, what have you to say to that?'

'Oh, mummy!' cheeped Teeny-weeny. 'Aren't we swallows wonderful!'

'No,' said his mother. 'Only God is wonderful. He tells us what to do and where to go, and without him we could do nothing. Without God, even the Man could do nothing—though he doesn't always realise it.'

Then the swallows all rose and went for a practice flight round the town, ready for their long journey to Spain.

WINSTON AND THE MIDGET MARROW

A story for town-dwelling juniors, by Caroline Somerville

Nothing was going right for Winston. He stood on the little balcony of the flat where he lived and stared miserably at a pot in the corner. In the pot was a marrow. It was the smallest marrow you could easily imagine—not much bigger than a rather thin sausage—and it wasn't growing any bigger, as far as Winston could see. As a marrow, it was a disaster.

Winston particularly wanted that marrow to grow. He'd been determined to produce a marrow for the school harvest festival ever since Mrs Miller, his class teacher, had first talked about it in the spring. 'I want you all to try to bring something that you've really taken trouble over,' she said. 'It can be a cake you've made or a scarf you've knitted or a plant you've grown in a pot, but I want it to have your hard work in it. Then it'll really mean something when we thank God for our harvest, and when we go round to the Old People's Home afterwards with the things we've brought, it'll mean something extra to them all that you've taken such trouble.'

Cakes and scarves, thought Winston scornfully. They weren't right for harvest festivals. Well, they might be right for Mrs Miller, but Winston knew what was what. He'd been to a harvest festival in a church last year, with his Gran, and he'd seen all the kids from the Sunday school take their gifts up to the vicar—and the coos and 'ahs' from the assembled mums had changed to a gasp of admiration as one boy (whose father had an allotment) staggered up the aisle under the weight of a marrow nearly as big as himself. As soon as Mrs Miller mentioned the word 'harvest', Winston's memory said, 'marrow!' He wasn't much good at reading or measuring things or making models—but something deep inside him told him that this was a job he *could* do . . . he could grow a splendid marrow.

And now it had all gone wrong and this miserable sausage in the pot was the result. Winston could have cried. He'd gone week after week to the Saturday market until he found a man

30

selling baby marrow plants; he'd had a stand-up row with his mum, who didn't want pots of earth on her nice clean balcony where the washing went; and when old Mrs Dolby's cat from next door had knocked over the pot, he had rushed out, bought a new one and swept up the mess before his mum got back and found out about it. No use. Winston sniffed, a long sad sniff, and then sniffed again.

'You look a bit down in the month, son,' said a voice. It was old Mr Dolby, on the next-door balcony. He was watering his row of geraniums. They looked unfairly green and healthy.

'It's this marrow,' said Winston. 'It won't grow.'

'Nay, I'm not surprised,' said Mr Dolby, peering over the dividing wall between the two balconies. 'Marrows like light, son. They like it warm. And they like food. What have you got in that pot, then—a bit of a scrape off the waste ground?'

'That's right,' said Winston, surprised. Where else was he to get soil?

'Well, marrows like muck,' said Mr Dolby firmly. 'Something they can get their teeth into, like. Horse-muck, that's what you want, lad. And get that plant into the light. Put a brick or two under it. Water it regular. But feed it first! You take my tip and find a horse.'

'Thanks, Mr Dolby!' said Winston. He grabbed his mum's orange plastic bucket from under the sink and shot out of the flats. He was halfway down the road before he stopped dead. Where, in the middle of this huge city, on a Saturday afternoon, was he going to find a horse? He tried the park. He tried the railway station. He roamed around the shopping streets, banging into busy women with his plastic bucket, getting shouted at by shoppers and jeered at by strange kids. It got later and later. His feet hurt.

Suddenly he was nearly knocked over by a great wave of boys, shouting and singing, all trailing red and white scarves and ribbons. The match was out—and by the look of it the home team had won. Winston realised with a start that he was right down by the football ground and being nearly flattened in the homegoing rush of the fans. Somebody barged into him hard and spun him round. His bucket went flying. There was an indignant scrape and clatter of hoofs.

Hoofs? Winston, battered and breathless, flung himself through the tide of fans to the edge of the pavement. Riding along the road, his big grey horse disdainfully sidestepping the orange bucket in its way, was a massive mounted policeman. He looked like somebody whose horse had nearly been hit by a bucket and who wanted to take the matter further.

Winston watched him. The fans disappeared, shouting, round a corner—leaving Winston alone with policeman, horse and bucket.

' Trying to score one on your own, were you ? ' said the policeman.

A few suitable replies shot into Winston's head—and he pushed them just as rapidly out again. This was no time for cheek! The only horse in perhaps twenty square miles was right here—within his grasp, not that he felt like grasping it.

' No, it wasn't nothing like that,' he mumbled. ' I wanted some of your horse's muck for my marrow, that's all.'

' For your grandma ? ' said the astonished policeman, who, being several feet above Winston's head, hadn't quite caught his explanation.

Patiently Winston sorted him out and told him the whole story, including Mr Dolby's advice.

' Quite right, too,' said the policeman. ' Knows his marrows, that friend of yours. I tell you what.' He took out his notebook, scribbled a message and gave the page to Winston. ' You take that to our stables in Firehouse Lane. Say I sent you—Sergeant James. You can take a number 17 bus there—but you'd best walk back home. All right ? '

' Right. Er—thanks,' muttered Winston. He retrieved his bucket and fled in the direction of the 17 bus.

There was another row when Winston's mum discovered the new, ripe contents of her orange plastic bucket—but Winston didn't care. He lovingly repotted his marrow and watched it grow. It grew almost as you watched it. Mr Dolby lent him a much bigger pot, and another trip to Firehouse Lane filled it. The marrow thrust out greedy roots and grew and grew. The holidays ended, school started again, harvest time came round—and the marrow went on growing.

' It's our harvest festival tomorrow, mum,' said Winston. ' I'm taking the marrow.'

' Getting that thing off my balcony, are you ? ' said his mum. ' Not before time! Funny—I'll almost miss it. You've got a right gift with plants, young Winston. Why not try a few tomatoes next year ? '

I might just do that, thought Winston, as he looked at his gigantic marrow, glowing amid the cakes and scarves and potted plants in the school hall. With a bit of help from Mr Dolby, and perhaps another visit to Firehouse Lane, and his mum's orange bucket. . . .

' All good gifts around us,' sang Winston at the top of his voice. You couldn't beat a *proper* harvest festival!

32

CREATOR OF THE HARVEST

Joyce and David Rowley linked their service to a theme which the children had previously explored

The Methodist church at Bignall End, Stoke-on-Trent has a mid-week meeting for its children, and for six weeks before the Harvest Festival the children thought about the various stages of the Creation story. During those sessions they painted pictures of plants, trees, grass, flowers, sun, moon, stars, fish, birds, reptiles, cattle and people, which were mounted on cards either 10" by 15" or 20" by 15". They also made a large 'Harvest Time' picture, about 6' by 4'. At the time of the service this was placed in the church porch, to welcome worshippers, but it could also be made the central item in the service and the other pictures placed around it.

A children's percussion group was formed to accompany the hymns and to provide incidental effects, and colour slides and recorded music were also used.

'AND GOD SAID'

Hymn: 'And God said' [*Come and Sing,* Scripture Union], with percussion accompaniment.

[*Church is darkened. Music from Grieg's 'Morning' is played, fading after about three minutes as narration starts*]

Narrator: In the beginning, when God made heaven and earth, the earth was without form and darkness covered emptiness.

[*Slow drum beat from group*]

Narrator: And God said:

Children: Let there be light.

[*Cymbals clash. Lights come on and off several times and then stay on*]

33

Narrator: And God let the mists separate to form the sky above and the oceans below. So God made the sky [*show sky slide*] and God made the seas [*show sea slide*]. And God said:

Children: Let the waters be gathered into one place so that dry land can appear.

Narrator: And God said:

Children: We will call the dry land earth [*show earth slide*]

Narrator: And God said:

Children: Let the earth produce plants, trees, grass and flowers. [*Children display their pictures and place them centrally, perhaps round the big harvest picture*]

Narrator: And God said:

Children: Let there be bright lights in the sky to give light to earth by day and night.
[*Sun, moon and star pictures are displayed*]

Narrator: And God said:

Children: Let the seas be full of fish [*fish pictures displayed*] and let the skies be full of birds of every kind [*bird pictures displayed*]

Narrator: And God said:

Children: Let there be animals, cattle, reptiles and wild life of every kind on the earth [*animal pictures displayed*]. [*Tambourines begin quietly and work up to a long crescendo*]

Narrator: And God said:

Children: Let us make man to be like us, someone who makes and who cares, the master of all life on earth. [*Display pictures of people*]. And so God made men and women.

Narrator: And he blessed them and gave them charge over the earth. He gives us that same responsibility today. [*A short address can follow here*]

Hymn: 'When God made creation' [*Sing to God*, SU] with percussion accompaniment.

This takes about ten minutes, but can, of course, be expanded with readings, hymns and intercessions into a full Harvest Festival service.

THE PROMISE OF THE RAINBOW

A harvest service described by Heather Wood

This is a Children's Harvest service we had in Haslingfield, a fairly small village with a United Sunday School of about 20 children. The children led this service at the Methodist chapel but brought their vegetables etc. to the parish church service a fortnight later. The chapel is very small and does not lend itself to large dramatisation but, usefully for this service, has a large plain semicircle in relief behind the pulpit, on which we stuck a rainbow made from crêpe paper.

The weeks prior to the service were used to enlarge the theme, ' God's promise is kept ', as symbolised in the rainbow. Children were generally familiar with the Noah story, so that was only briefly re-capped, to lead to the meaning of the rainbow promise, with special reference to seedtime and harvest in the whole world. (Genesis 8. 20–22, *NEB*). The work was varied for the different age groups.

WEEK 1

The ability of plants to grow in surprising places and with all sorts of handicaps. We had local examples of weeds poking through a recently made tarmac footpath and a giant sunflower in full bloom from a crack at the edge of a pavement. (Actually I first had this idea from a plant seen on holiday, growing vigorously through the top of a heap of rubble. This was also described.) Mention was also made of willowherb growing on bomb sites and building sites.

The younger children drew pictures at home of any plant they had found in an odd place and they made a collage of my holiday plant. At this point we introduced the reading we would have from the New Testament. Mark 4. 26–29, *TEV*. Older children started to think about farming in many overseas countries, where farmers expect, and often do get, harvest from soil and conditions we would not think at all favourable. We started to learn a new hymn, ' Lord of the Harvest ' (*Faith, Folk and Festivity*, page 24).

WEEK 2

The youngest children started to make 'rainbow flowers' from tissue paper, cutting out lots of circles. (In the end these were mainly made up by their teacher and her teenage daughter as one was needed for every expected member of the congregation, also fitting them together proved too fiddly for the little ones and inadvisable because of the wire.)

To make flowers: Cut out circles in varying sizes from 6" to 2" diameter in tissue paper of all the rainbow colours. Some circles can be folded into quarters and petals shaped. If you wish to be strict about the order the petal colours are in, have all the largest circles in violet and all the smallest red, or vice-versa, but it is more economical to mix the colours. Place seven different coloured petals on top of each other and twist florist's wire through the centres, making a stalk. These look very effective when all placed in a container.

The Juniors either wrote about a plant growing in difficult conditions or else wrote 'rainbow poems'. These were asked to be on the theme of seedtime and harvest, with the first letter of each line being the initial letters of the rainbow colours in order, either VIBGYOR or ROYGBIV. I wrote an example to help them get the idea and they finished them at home. (This project went down very well with this particular class, but I could not have done it in previous years.) Others also wrote prayers for inclusion in the service.

The Senior group made a poster to illustrate how the effects of natural disasters—flood, drought, earthquake—can be used to help people to a new start, with new and better stock, seeds, irrigation and of course the scientific help which is available especially on such occasions. Our hymn 'Lord of the Harvest' illustrated this point very well. The poster was made from pictures cut from missionary, Oxfam and similar pamphlets. Since this age group is quite well aware that sometimes God's promise does seem to fail, the aim here was to emphasise that when crops fail in one part of the world, other parts not only have sufficient to share but also have the technical skills to develop longterm plans that can reduce the effects of crop failure. (The Honduras hurricane happened at this time so we brought this into our discussions, and also sent a donation to the appeal fund.)

WEEK 3

Final preparations for the service. Seven youngest Primary children were dressed in simple tunics and hats made of crêpe paper in the seven rainbow colours. They would march on, in order, at two points in the Service and stand in a line. We also learned (from memory!) the first few lines of the old pop song 'I can sing a rainbow'.

Two Primaries, who could read if they practised, learnt to read two simple poems, 'A Play of Colours' by P. C. McAll (*Poems for School Assemblies and other occasions*, edited by D. M. Prescott—a much recommended book) and 'Where' by Natalie Joan (*Treasures of English Verse*, OUP—possibly now out of print). Hopes of recorders to accompany the new hymn were dashed as players became ill or couldn't attend, so a friend was enlisted to accompany on guitar. The visiting preacher had been primed about the theme and the work we had done. Hymns were chosen for their connection with the theme, and the children's prayers were augmented by the prayer 'Our Daily Bread' from the Ladybird Book of *Prayers Through the Year*. Every child had something to do in the service.

ORDER OF SERVICE

Introduction (Teacher): The theme of our service is 'God's promise is kept', as symbolised in the rainbow. We will start by hearing how God made that promise (a Covenant it is called in the Bible), to Noah, after the great and devastating flood.

[*March on the 'rainbow' children, to stand in front during Reading*]

Reading (Senior): Genesis 8. 20–22, 9. 8–14.

Hymn: 'Come ye thankful people, come'.

Prayers: The children's own, and from the Ladybird book.

The Lord's prayer

Hymn (children and guitar): 'Lord of the Harvest' (FF and F).

Introduction (Teacher) to poems, etc. by children:

As our hymn said, we must not forget that while we can thank God for our harvest and plentiful food, there are some parts of the world with which we must share our plenty. Only these last few days we have heard of the hurricane in Honduras which has destroyed nearly all the banana harvest. One of our posters on the wall shows how, in spite of starvation and floods, these disasters sometimes give new opportunities not only for people to get new homes and conditions, but also for us to share our scientific and technical knowledge; God's promise that the harvest shall never completely cease can be seen to be true. Other pictures here show how plants grow well in most peculiar places—for that matter we should probably be astonished at the soil condition in which some farmers in some parts of the world have to grow their crops. We are now going to hear some poems and stories about the harvest. The first poems were written by three different girls, though Karen will read them all. They are written so that the first line begins with the initial letter of the colours of the rainbow in order. Natasha has written a story about a plant which actually prefers its hard mountain home—and finally we shall hear a parable Jesus told of how God makes the seeds grow and bring us their harvest.

[*March on ' rainbow '*]

Rainbow poems:

Reap the harvest
Over again.
Your harvest is coming
Get ready now.
But soon
It will be going,
Very, very soon.

(Karen Burtenshaw, 8½)

Rainbow
On the hillside
Yellow, blue and green.
Green grass growing all around
Blue sky above the dew is seen
In our harvest is a rainbow
Violet, indigo and blue.

(Alison Wood, 8½)

Very windy
It's harvest time,
Bread is made from the corn.
God makes everything.
Your cereals are made from wheat.
Our farmers have been very busy this month
Rabbits roam in the corn.

(Stephanie Godsell, 8)

Poem: ' Where '

Poem: ' A Play of Colours '

38

Story: 'The Plant'

Once there was a plant. It was strange. It lived on the mountain. And it was peaceful there. But one day a big girl came and picked it. She said to her Mummy 'I am going to take this home'. But when she had it all winter it started to die out. So next summer she put it back. (Natasha Wilson, 6)

[*March off the 'rainbow'*]

Reading: Mark 4. 26–29, *TEV*

Hymn: 'All things which live below the sky' (Methodist Hymn Book 852)

Notices, Collection: (taken by two non-reading primary boys)

Prayer: (Preacher)

Hymn: 'Lord of all being, throned afar' (MHB 32)

Address

Rainbow flowers were distributed by the children to all the congregation—after the fashion of 'Flower Power' of a few years ago.

Hymn: 'We plough the fields and scatter' (MHB 963)

Blessing

Readers who like the idea of a Rainbow Service may find the picture of Noah in *Old Testament Pictures for Today* (CIO) useful as a source of inspiration for a frieze. They may also wish to refer to page 21 of this book for the hymn by Caroline Somerville, 'God Almighty set a rainbow'.

Useful addresses for posters, etc.:
Oxfam, Education Dept., 274 Banbury Road, Oxford.

Christian Aid, Schools Dept., 2 Sloane Gardens, London SW1W 9BW.

'OUR FAVOURITE THINGS'

The children of Margaret Williams' infant school in Swindon built up through assemblies to their harvest service—which they shared

The main idea we were trying to get over to the children was that God provides our food and he wants us to share what he provides.

DAY 1

In Assembly the children were asked to think what their favourite food was—we told them some of the possibilities and asked a few of the children if they had already decided on their favourite food.

The children then went back and discussed this in their class-rooms. Some children made pictures of the food they enjoyed eating most of all while others wrote about it. Others looked through magazines to see if there were pictures of their favourite food amongst the advertisements.

DAY 2

The next day the teachers had chosen two children from each class to show their pictures or read their writing (these were chosen so as to give a variety of food, not to have 'baked beans' from everyone!). All the other children who had produced something brought in their pieces of work and each class held up its work to show the others. All this was to be stuck on to a long piece of frieze paper for the hall. After the couple from each class had read or showed their favourite food, the source of the food was traced back and in each case we found that God, the provider of all our food, had made it possible for us to enjoy this food.

The children were then asked to close their eyes and make a picture in their minds of the food they like best and while they were doing this a prayer of thanks was said to God.

DAY 3

In the meantime the children had taken letters home asking for gifts of food for the harvest festival. These were being brought during the week and kept in their classrooms until today, when they were arranged in the hall. The children then came back into the hall later in the morning for the harvest festival service. (To this service the people of the local old people's home nearby were invited and although only about a dozen managed to come it is something which they always eagerly look forward to. It also means that the whole school can actually see what is going to happen to the gifts.) According to the number of old folk who were there, an appropriate number of boxes of food were made up for children to give them one each at the end of the service. Each class made a contribution of a song or a poem to the service and some of the older children had written their own prayers for it which they read out. The service started with the theme of saying 'thank you'—that we all, whether we are 5 or 85, we still need to say thank you to God. It ended with the idea of sharing what God has given us, and each of the older visitors was given a box containing harvest gifts.

DAY 4

The remainder of the harvest gifts were divided up into boxes for the old folk who could not come to the service. These boxes were transported to the old people's home by the staff and then some of the children were taken there and they went around the people's bed-sitters, giving them the parcels of food.

A WEEK OF HARVEST ASSEMBLIES

An idea by Alice Goodman for junior school worship

We are accustomed to protracted celebrations at Christmas in schools, and to a lesser extent before Easter. Harvest, however, usually is dismissed at one Assembly, when the produce which the children may have been asked to bring to school is received in traditional style.

However, the theme of Harvest is found in various places in the Bible, and using some of these, it is possible to have a series of Assemblies, linked by the theme, which can last at least for five days.

Many schools nowadays have times when different classes are responsible for School Assemblies by pre-arrangement. The Harvest theme is a very suitable one for this scheme. Five different classes can be responsible for its total production, and each, after preliminary staff consultation, can work alone.

Here are a few suggestions. There are, of course, others one can find in the Bible.

1. God's promise to Noah that harvest will not cease

This theme is generally very popular, and the younger classes enjoy acting the story. Much can be done by mime, while the story is told by several children acting as narrators. An alternative is to organize the preparation by having a series of pictures, which must of course, be large, and as the story unfolds, these may be shown one by one, till a complete ' series ' is displayed. In any event, sufficient time must be given so that the class has time to prepare and discuss. No teacher likes to be ' rushed '.

2. The Story of Ruth

This story also is a popular one with the children, The book of Ruth is short, only four chapters, and with a modern translation the children will soon know the story, and be ready to consider how best to present it. Similar methods to those already described

42

are well-tried and generally successful. It should be noted that in the very first verse, we are reminded of the famine conditions that often occurred, and how people were obliged to go to where food was available.

3. The Story of Joseph

This is a long story, and it is essential not to make it tedious in consequence. It is best to concentrate on the last part, ' pulling together ' the first part by means of narration. For example, several children could narrate between them how Joseph was left in the pit, and later sold into slavery by his brothers, how he made himself indispensable to Potiphar, but later was thrown into prison.

The story might begin with Joseph fetched out of prison to interpret Pharaoh's dreams, with the reminder that he had already proved this ability with the interpretation of the dreams of his fellow-servants.

The dreams interpreted, he now had to convince the people of the urgent need to save for the famine of the future. Children can be placed in different parts of the hall, miming the coming from far with harvest produce in the good years for storage. At last, famine settles in and Jacob is forced to send his sons to buy corn in Egypt.

Again, the use of children placed in the hall serves to indicate the distances travelled, and very good use can be made of mime.

The last two days can be used to present two of the Harvest parables told by Jesus.

4. The parable of the sower

Again, this can be told by a mixture of narration, mime, and picture display. If pictures are much used, the children can work in groups beforehand, making a large picture of each type of ground where the seed fell, and the results as it attempted to grow. As each picture is displayed, members of the group involved explain it to the school.

5. The parable of the rich man who would not share

This is a good story to finish the week with because it is short, and therefore can, if you wish, be combined very well with the general bringing of Harvest produce as an offering for the needy. The story is found in Luke 12.

The class involved in this day's Assembly might be an older class who can plan how the offering of the produce might be made. A collection of pictures from ' Oxfam ' or similar organizations stresses the need for sharing the resources we have, even in today's affluence.

'ALL GOOD GIFTS'

A harvest service for primary schools by Alan F. Davies

Opening music: ' Food, glorious food ' (from the musical *Oliver*)

Hymn: Any favourite harvest hymn.
[*The items which follow can be linked by a musical theme, perhaps a verse of this hymn played by piano or recorder group between each item.*]

Narrator: We have just been singing together a harvest hymn—a hymn of thanksgiving. Just in case we are wondering what we are being thankful about, perhaps we can find out together. Perhaps we already know—but let's make sure. For instance . . .

1st Child: [*shows apple*] Apples could have come from several places. Bright red ones from Australia, maybe, or from Italy, or around Worcester, or from your garden. Many people think that English apples are the best—but wherever they come from, the trees have to be pruned and sprayed to prevent disease. The apples have to be picked, graded and packed for market, and sold. Quite a lot of people could have helped to bring us apples. . . .

2nd Child: [*picks up orange*] . . . or this. How many of you have large orange trees in your gardens? No, of course not. Oranges won't grow out of doors in our country. Nor will lemons, nor grapefruit (picks these up). They come from across the sea, where it is hot enough to ripen them, picked and packed by people we shall never meet. But thank you all the same!

3rd Child: Just look at this basket of harvest food [*holds it up*]. It's almost like a map of the world. [*Gives names of places where foods come from.*]

4th Child: [*picks up some coal*] Have you thought of this as part of our harvest? Coal? Well, it is. Without it many of our factories would have to close—and many of our homes and schools would have to close. So—old King Coal—welcome to our harvest!

44

5th Child [*picks up plate of fish*]*:* And welcome to these, too. They were caught in the deep sea, perhaps in a gale, with the sea breaking over the boat from waves twenty feet high. So let's not forget the fishermen.

6th Child: Many of the gifts are given to us so that we can use them. With coal, as we have just said, we can make fire. We can do that with wood too . . . or we can just enjoy trees in all their colours as the seasons pass . . . or we can make things from them—like furniture.

7th Child: And there's ordinary water, which we use in so many ways, and without which we could not even stay alive! [*Holds up glass of water.*] Think about that—without it we couldn't stay alive . . .

8th Child: Here is another very important part of the harvest [*shows bag of flour*]. Perhaps not so long ago this flour was growing as wheat in an English field. One fine day it was harvested, and the grain was ground into flour. Some of it was sold to us like this in shops, but a very great deal of our flour is made into bread for us [*holds up loaf*]. In Bible times it was done like this:

9th Child [*reads*]*:* ' He looked, and there at his head was a cake baked on hot stones, and a pitcher of water.' (I Kings 19.6).

10th Child [*holds up harvest loaf, with small loaves and fish upon it*]*:* This is also bread, made into a special harvest loaf, which also tells a very old story:

11th Child [*reads*] the story of the Feeding of the Five Thousand (Mark 6. 31–46), perhaps from *New World* by Alan T. Dale (Oxford).

10th Child: . . . and here are the loaves and fishes to remind us of the way in which Christ fed his people. And now God still feeds us, through the harvest of food we eat, through his love for us.

[*Choir sing a suitable anthem or folksong.*]

12th Child: Because of this, bread has always had a rather special importance. Every Sunday, in churches all over the country, God reminds us of his love for us, through bread and wine in the Holy Communion service.

[*Places in position plate of bread and bottle of wine.*]

13th Child [*reads*]*:* I Corinthians 23–26 from *New World* (p. 291 of paperback edition ?), beginning ' On the night. . .'.

Hymn: ' Jesus, good above all other ' or another suitable.

14th Child: Jesus shares this love with all of us—another kind of harvest, really. Does this make any difference to us? I ask you again—does this make any difference to us? It is part of God's plan that everyone shall have a fair share, but it is our job to see that they do. Those who have enough, like us, have to feed the hungry—and there are far many more than 5,000 hungry today!

15th Child: ' Before the loaf comes the flour,
Before the flour comes the mill,
Before the mill comes the wheat, the rain and the sun,
Before all this comes the Father's will.'

Jesus said, ' Give *us*,' not ' *me* ' ' our daily bread.'

[*Enter child dressed to look obviously in great need, who comes from back, down central aisle, sits in pre-arranged spot:*]

Needy Child [*imploringly*]: ' Give us this day our daily bread.'

Hymn and Offertory.

Prayers.

Blessing.

HARVEST TIME

A sketch in rhyme
by Ivy Russell

A trestle table across the back of the acting area holds tins of food and other items that might be seen in a shop.
> [*Enter Mother, left, carrying a shopping basket*]

Mother: I am a mother, who walks down the street
Choosing the food for my children to eat.
> [*She goes slowly across to right, looking at the food as she goes*]
> [*Enter shopman, left, wearing an apron*]

Shopman: This is a shop where the shelves are piled high
With packets and bottles for mother to buy,
As, holding her basket, she walks down the street
Choosing the food for her children to eat.
> [*Shopman crosses to position behind counter*]
> [*Enter farmer, left, carrying a gardening tool*]

Farmer: I am the farmer who rises at dawn
To plough up my fields or to harvest my corn,
To make all the loaves that are piled up so high,
The cakes and the biscuits for mother to buy,
As, holding her basket, she walks down the street,
Choosing the food for her children to eat.
> [*Farmer crosses to right*]
> [*Enter dairymaid, wearing white apron and carrying bucket*]

Dairymaid: I am the dairymaid, first out of bed,
Milking the cows in their freshly-cleaned shed.
I send you cheeses, and butter piled high
In neat little packets for mother to buy,
As, holding her basket, she walks down the street,
Choosing the food for her children to eat.
> [*Dairymaid crosses to right*]
> [*Enter fisherman, wearing navy sweater and boots*]

Fisherman: I am a fisherman, out with the fleet,
Bringing back mackerel and herrings so sweet,
Cod in the freezer, and pilchards piled high
In tins on the counter for mother to buy,
As, holding her basket, she walks down the street,
Choosing the food for her children to eat.
[*Fisherman crosses to right*]
[*Enter tea-picker, wearing a sari*]

Tea-picker: I am a picker, from over the sea,
Gathering leaves that will give you your tea.
Tea comes in packets, which now are piled high
On shelves at the grocer's, for mother to buy,
As, holding her basket, she walks down the street,
Choosing the food for her children to eat.
[*All characters now come to front in a line*]

All: So thank you, dear God, for the farmer at home,
For all the brave fishermen out on the foam,
And everyone working beneath the blue sky
To send us the food for our mothers to buy,
As, holding her basket, she walks down the street,
Choosing the food for her children to eat.
[*As they say the last two lines they separate, and walk off each side*]

(Reprinted by kind permission of *Child Education*)

WORKERS WITH GOD

Rodney Pope suggests a big, child-constructed frieze as a visual aid for his harvest service

This address needs the maximum co-operation from the children and will probably be practicable only where there is either a church school or a large Sunday school.

Individual children should make drawings of specific items to be used to build up a frieze during the harvest service. Guidance should be given as to the appropriate size required and suitable sized pieces of paper provided. Older children will enjoy drawing the bigger items such as ploughs and combine harvesters, whilst younger ones will easily manage rain clouds, sunshine and wheat in various stages of growth. Weather should be shown as appropriate, with heavy grey rainclouds, snowflakes and sunbeams getting larger and brighter throughout the summer months.

A background should be prepared for the frieze, from news-print, sugar paper or old wallpaper, and before the service this should be fixed either to the wall or some other convenient place where it can be easily seen by all.

The paper should be divided into 12 vertical sections, each space clearly marked with a month of the year from October to September—see diagram attached.

Prepare sufficient copies of the prayer of St Ignatius Loyola for distribution to adults and children of junior school age and above. Appropriate reading: Mark 4. 26–29, which can be used at the beginning of the service.

Many of you have been working hard to help us with our service today. You will see that I have prepared a large wall chart, marked out into the months of the year. When I call out each month, its weather and what happens then, I should like those of you who have drawn these pictures to bring them out and (Mr......Mrs......Miss......) will help you to fix them in the right place.

Drawings required for Frieze of Winter Wheat, showing Months in which they should be placed

October	November	December	January	February	March	April	May	June	July	August	September
Rain	Rain	Frost	Frost	Rain	Rain	Rain	Sun	Sun	Sun	Sun	Sun
						Sunshine		S h o w e r s			
Ploughing Sowing	Sprouting	Sleeping Plants	Sleeping Plants	First True Leaves	Growing Plants	Growing Plants	Ears form	Ears filling out	Ripening	Combining	To Mill
				Rolling	Harrow- ing	Spraying					
				Harrow- ing	Spraying	Fertilis- ing					
					Fertilising						

(This is but a brief outline and could be made much more detailed if required.)

50

(The list of required drawings is now slowly read through, in order, and, if several helpers are available, the actual placing of the drawings in their correct places should not take long.)

October—Rain: Ploughing and sowing
November to January—Rain and frost: Sprouting
February—Rain: First real leaves—rolling, harrowing
March—Rain: Growing plants, harrowing, spraying, fertilising
April—Rain and sunshine: Growing plants, spraying, fertilising
May—Sun: Ears begin to form
June—Sun and showers: Ears filling out
July—Sun and showers: Ripening
August—Sun: Combine harvesting
September—Sun: Grain transported to flour mill.

There we are, there is our completed frieze and without your help it would not have been possible. *Together* we have produced a very reasonable chart showing how we get the wheat from which we make our daily bread.

Just as we had to work together to build up the picture, so the farmer has to work with God to produce the harvest. That is what Jesus taught in the lesson which we heard read. (It's only very short, so perhaps you will not mind if I read it again?)

It is God who puts the life into the seed, it is God who provides the right weather conditions. If the seed is without life, if the weather is unsuitable, then no matter how hard the farmer works his crop will be a failure. On the other hand the crop will be equally poor if the farmer does not do his work properly too.

What is true of the harvest is true of everything that we do: God gives us all the ingredients which are needed for success, but he expects us to work as hard as we can with him in order to produce the very best results. It is God and us together. *(Teachers can compare I Cor. 3. 5b–9)*

In front of you, you will find copies of a prayer composed by a great Christian, Ignatius Loyola, a prayer in which we ask God's help to work hard for him in his world. Let us say that prayer together now, and then you might like to take it home with you and use it every day.

' Teach us, good Lord, to serve thee as thou deservest; to give and not to count the cost; to fight and not to heed the wounds; to toil and not to seek for rest; to labour and not to ask for any reward, save that of knowing that we do thy will; through Jesus Christ Our Lord, Amen.'

'WE DEPEND ON GOD—
AND ON EACH OTHER'

A project explored by Margaret Williams' Sunday school, which could lend itself to day school use

The aim of this project was to show our dependence upon God and our dependence upon other people. There were two weeks of preparation and then the project culminated in the Harvest Thanksgiving in church.

WEEK 1. THE IMPORTANCE OF WATER

For this week we used seeds and little pots of soil and a plant such as a Busy Lizzie. We started in our groups by discussing the packets of seeds shown, some large, some as fine as dust. From these seeds plants of various kinds will grow—some into bean plants about 6–8 feet tall, some into cress which is no more than about 2 inches high. We thought why the seeds did not start to grow in their packets: because of the things needed to make them germinate, one of which is water. Having germinated, they needed water to go on growing. Just in case anyone might have any doubts about this we carried out some simple experiments. Into pots of *dry* soil we planted cress seeds. Some children were to take these home and water them each day. The other children were to take theirs home and not give them any water at all. We looked at these when the children returned them the following week.

We also looked at a house plant (a Busy Lizzie is good for this) and we took it home and did not water it for a week so that the children could see what happened to plants that were denied water. So we concluded that plants need water and so do we. We pointed out that our bodies can go without food for a longer time than they can go without water; without water they become dehydrated, and in that state we cannot live long. We are told that a high percentage of our bodies consists of water and we are constantly losing water through perspiration, so it has to be replaced. We cannot live without water.

We then thought of where all the water comes from. Get children to trace back to the source of our water; they might do a diagram showing wind rising off the sea, clouds forming over hills, rain falling from the clouds to make streams, growing to rivers which run back into the sea.

We thought how no one has been able to make rain clouds yet. Only God, the Creator who has ordered these things, can bring rain clouds and rain. In some countries where they are short of rain, scientists have succeeded in making the clouds drop rain occasionally but no one can make the actual rain clouds. So we are dependent upon God for our water.

For the next part of the lesson we thought how this water comes to our houses. The children were able to tell how the water was stored in reservoirs (let children find out, if not already known, the reservoir which supplies their water) and then piped to their houses. It would be very inconvenient in towns of our size if we all had to walk to a well or to a river each day for our water. So we are dependent to a large extent on other people to get water to our houses—technicians, plumbers and many others.

In our harvest service we wanted to make the congregation realise how important water was, so we discussed ways in which we might do this. This following were ideas suggested by the children:

1. By telling the congregation about our experiments;
2. By tape-recording sounds of water such as a tap running, water running out of a bath, waterfall or river; the sound of the sea;
3. By making up prayers thanking God for water.

Children then started to prepare this part of the service, by making up prayers and discussing or doing the tape recording.

Before we went home, we put a tile on the grass outside so that some of the grass would be without light for a week.

WEEK 2. THE IMPORTANCE OF SUNLIGHT

After looking at the pots of seeds and plants returned from last week, the children were taken outside to a corner of the grass where a square tile had been placed a week ago. This was lifted and we saw what had happened the grass. (If this is impossible, then grow some grass seeds in a pot and leave it in the dark when they have grown.) The importance of sunlight to plants was discussed. We then thought how dependent we were upon sunlight. We asked the children to suggest what the sun did for us and had suggestions such as 'the sun gives us daylight', 'the sun gives us sunburn', 'the sun gives us warmth', 'the sun warms the sea so that we can swim in it in summertime'.

It was decided to do experiments similar to last week's with the cress seeds. The same pots of cress were to be taken home—this time some of them were to be kept in a dark place and some in a very sunny place, and the following week we would see what had happened to them. Discussion followed as to why some parts of the world were hotter than others and the difference this made to the kinds of plants which grew there and the types of animals which lived there.

We proceeded to think of our sources of warmth in wintertime and discovered that these sources would not be available to us if it were not for the existence of the sun. The sun is the source of our heat and energy in their various forms. We are, therefore, absolutely dependent upon God who has created the sun. The fuels we use, however, are only available to us through the help of other people. We depend on other people to dig the coal out of the ground, to drill for oil under the desert or beneath the sea and we rely on other people to pipe the gas to our homes. So we are dependent upon other people.

The remainder of this week was devoted to planning the service for the next week, one group of children thinking of hymns to sing, one group writing some more prayers and another group of children working out how they would tell the congregation about these two weeks of preparation.

HARVEST SERVICE

Opening Hymn: 'We plough the fields and scatter'.

Child then tells the congregation that our aim in harvest service is to try and show our dependence upon God and our dependence upon other people. First, everyone is going to listen to part of a psalm.

Group of children read from Psalm 136 (NEB version) verses 1–9 and verses 25 and 26, the verses being read by individual children of the group while they read the recurring words ' his love endures for ever ' together as a group.

One child then tells the congregation that we wish them to listen to some sounds they have tape recorded.

The tape-recording of running water, water being emptied from the bath, the sound of the sea, is played and then some children proceed to describe the experiments they did in Week 1, proving that we cannot live without God's gift of rain. They end their dialogue by saying together:

' We depend on God for our water and we depend on other people to get it to us.'

Hymn: 'All things bright and beautiful'.

In silence a child goes up to the pulpit and lights a candle and says 'Light'. That child comes down and another goes up, holds up a torch, switches it on and says 'Light'. Another child goes up and holds a sparkler to the candle until it lights. After the sparkler has died away the child says 'Light'. Another child switches on a projector light up in the pulpit and says 'Light'. This last child then tells the congregation that we are now going to think of God's gift of light.

Other children then tell of their findings during Week 2 and how we cannot live without God's gift of sunlight. They end their dialogue by saying together:

'We depend on God for the source of our warmth and light and we depend on other people to harness it for us.'

All the infant children then sing together the three verses of 'We praise you for the sun' (*Someone's Singing, Lord*).

Prayers were then read out by children who had composed them last week.

Hymn (during which Harvest gifts were taken up to the altar): 'Praise, O praise our God and King'.

Talk by the Vicar, picking up the points made by the children.

Closing Hymn: 'Praise and thanksgiving, Father, we offer'. *(100 Hymns for Today)*

'THIS IS OUR HARVEST'

A service for primary schools, which is also suitable for church use, by Alan F. Davies

It is suggested that the introductory reading be written out and decorated by a child before the service. It can be mounted on card so that it can be placed with some ceremony on the display of produce. For continuity, the words 'This is our harvest' should be said by the same child. A commentary on the meaning of the processions can be given as the service proceeds.

Opening music

Call to worship: Psalm 150 [*choral speech or sung with percussion accompaniment*].

Hymn: 'We plough the fields and scatter.'

Child: ' This is our harvest '

[*Enter procession of children carrying harvest produce. They make their offerings during the reading. These are accepted by the priest or teacher taking the service and fitted into the harvest display previously arranged—gaps having been left for this purpose.*]

Reading: Deuteronomy 26, 1–4 and 10–11.

Child: ' This is our harvest.'

[*Enter procession of children carrying the harvest of their own work: writing, pictures, needlework, original poems, models, etc. which are placed in the appointed spot. A harvest hymn or anthem can be sung here.*]

Child: ' This is our harvest.'

[*Enter procession in which children bring to the front, or to the altar, a prayer book, Bible, child's own book of prayers, etc.*]

Prayer taken from the book used in the procession.

Reading: Psalm 104. 10–24 (read from the Bible used in the procession).

Child: ' This is our harvest.'

[*Enter procession carrying bread, water, wine and, if thought suitable, a chalice. These are received and placed in a central position.*]

Child: ' This is our harvest.'

[*Enter procession bringing offerings of money for some suitable charity, which are also placed in a central position. The commentary at this point should emphasise the harvest of ' caring and sharing '.*]

Reading: I Corinthians 13. 1–8 and 13.

Prayers (including some by children).

Hymn: ' Let us with a gladsome mind.'

Blessing.

Closing music.

GOD'S FAMILY

The idea of interdependence graphically shown during a family service address by Rodney Pope

You will need: A large map of the world (Mercator projection) or a large globe; some masking tape painted a bright colour, or coloured Sellotape; cornflakes, bread, butter, orange marmalade, tea or coffee, sugar, milk, water.

It may look from the goods on the table as if they were chosen at random from the shelves of the supermarket. However, if you look a little more closely it will be seen that they are typical of the sort of things we eat and drink when we have a fairly simple breakfast—cornflakes, bread, butter and marmalade, tea, or coffee, milk and sugar.

These products are so easy to buy that it is easy to forget just how far many of them have to travel to reach us, and how many people have to co-operate to bring them to us. We could get a better idea if we were to stick a piece of coloured tape on this map (globe) to represent the places from which our breakfast may have come. *Here the children should be asked to make suggestions of the likely place of origin of the several items and to stick pieces of coloured masking tape on the map as appropriate. For instance:*

Cornflakes	*USA*
Bread (wheat)	*Canada*
Marmalade (oranges)	*Israel, Spain*
Tea	*Sri Lanka*
Coffee	*Brazil*
Sugar	*West Indies*
Butter	*New Zealand*
Milk	*Cheshire*
Water	*local*

Thank you all for your help; now we have a map-picture which shows how far our provisions have to travel and also that many people in so many countries, and in so many different ways, need to work together to provide us with even the simplest meal. There will be not only those engaged in farming crops but those engaged in transport, research, marketing, providing machinery and equipment. The list of jobs likely to be involved would be enormous—I wonder how many you can suggest in just sixty seconds?

Well, it is easy to see from that impressive list that we are all one great family who need each other; only by working together, by each giving of his best in the work which he has to do, can the many varied needs of all that family be met. Jesus taught us that, as members of God's one family, we should pray for each others needs to be met—' Our Father . . . Give US each day our daily bread '—but how can we make that prayer more real? How can we help to make it really relevant to daily life?

First, by looking at work in the right way, understanding it as a personal gift to the needs of God's world-wide family. ' To work is to pray,' said St Augustine, and work seen as the service of God's family is real active prayer.

Secondly, we might try using an atlas as a prayer book, turning one page each day. For the youngest, the daily prayer could be a very simple one, such as, ' God bless the people in this country '; others might find it helpful to place a loose sheet of thin paper between each page, noting on it from time to time events or people especially to be remembered in that particular country. So shall we pray regularly for all the members of God's family throughout the world—the family upon whom we depend for our daily food? *(In schools an atlas could be used in this way for morning assembly.)*

THE HARVEST EUCHARIST

At the church Festival service, Rodney Pope explores the new, deeper meaning given by Jesus to the Harvest symbols among which he had grown to manhood

You will need: Fifteen children or young people willing to help (who may either read their short pieces or memorise them); cross, two candles, bread, wine, water, two 'lulavs' (see below), two oranges. The 'lulavs' should be made from materials as close to the original as possible.

Narrator: Instead of preaching a sermon this morning, I should like to explain to you the meaning of the procession which will take place during the Offertory hymn, in a few moments' time. I have asked those who will be taking part in the procession to come out here and explain what they will be carrying and the meaning of its symbolism.

Thanksgiving for the harvest has been happening almost since man's history began, and by the time of Jesus the great Jewish festival of the Ingathering—or Feast of the Tabernacles, as it is sometimes called—was already centuries old. This festival, which lasted eight days, was not only a thanksgiving for harvest but also a commemoration of the great Israelite escape from captivity in Egypt under the leadership of Moses; and it was also a looking forward to the anticipated coming of the kingdom of the Messiah. Let (John) take up the story . . .

[Children with 'lulavs' come forward]

1st child: Most pilgrims to the festival in Jerusalem carried in their right hands a bunch of palm, myrtle and willow which was tied around with a golden thread. This was called a 'lulav', and was waved during the service.

2nd child: This was a reminder of the wanderings of the Exodus —palms representing the valleys and plains, willows a plentiful water supply, and myrtles the trees and shrubs on high ground.

[*Children with citrus fruits come forward*]

3rd child: In his left hand the pilgrim carried a citrus fruit, which was called an ' ethrog '.

4th child: This was a token which stood for the wonderful fruits of the harvest of the Promised Land.

[*Young people carrying water come forward*]

5th child: Every day, during the eight days of the feast, a priest brought the golden pitcher, containing a little more than a quart of water from the Pool of Siloam. This was poured out at the foot of the altar.

6th child: This was an act of thanksgiving for the gift of rain which produced the crops, and a looking forward to the outpouring of the Holy Spirit in the coming kingdom of the Messiah.

[*Young people carrying candles come forward*]

7th child: The whole temple was a blaze of light from the four great golden candlesticks and many flaming torches.

8th child: These symbolised the light of the glory of God.

Narrator: St John tells us that on the last day of one of these festivals (' The Great Day ': John 7. 37–52; 8. 12) Jesus himself came and joined in the ceremonies. Here in person, was the Messiah who was to bring about a deliverance far greater than that of the Exodus, who was himself the Light of the world, and who offered water not from the Pool of Siloam but from the well of Eternal Life. So he called out to those who were busy celebrating the Harvest Thanksgiving.

' If anyone is thirsty let him come to me . . . I am the Light of the World.'

[*Enter child with cross*]

9th child: So as at their harvest the Jews gave thanks for the deliverance of the Exodus, we, at our festival, give thanks for our deliverance from sin by Jesus. This cross is our symbol of victory.

[*Enter children with water and candles*]

10th child: Water is symbolic of the new life offered by Jesus.

11th child: These candles symbolise Jesus, the Light of the world, the Messiah of God.

Narrator: So the old Harvest Thanksgiving of the Feast of the Tabernacles was given a new and deeper meaning by Jesus himself. The emphasis changed from the needs of the body to the deeper needs of man's whole being—the Living Food for those who hunger and thirst after righteousness.

[Enter children with bread]

12th child: Jesus said, ' He who comes to me will never be hungry ' (*John 6. 35*).

13th child: Jesus took bread, gave thanks to God, broke it and said, ' This is my Body which is for you: Do this as a memorial of me.' *(I Cor. 11–24).*

[Enter children with wine]

14th child: Jesus said, ' He who believes in me shall never be thirsty '. *(John 4. 14).*

15th child: Jesus took the cup of wine and said, ' This is the new covenant in my blood; whenever you drink it do this as a memorial of me '. (I Cor. 11. 25).

Narrator: So then in this Harvest Eucharist (or 'Thanksgiving', for that is what the Greek word ' eucharist ' means) we give thanks to God not only for our daily food which sustains our daily life, but also for the promise of a new life with Jesus. We are giving thanks for the food which he gives us to strengthen that new life, through the bread and wine which he blesses when we remember him in this special way.

As this procession makes its way to the Sanctuary, during the singing of the Offertory hymn, led by the cross of the Saviour, and the symbols of the Light of the world, give thanks to God in your heart for the magnificence of all his gifts. They are not just for our bodies but for our minds and hearts and feelings, too. Thank you, Lord!

CREATION: A Bible Study

The caring Creator, who loves the world he made, is the theme of our worship. Dr Edgar Jones looks at the unique affirmations of the biblical teaching concerning creation

In the whole literature of the Ancient Near East we find that the peoples of Sumer, Babylon and Egypt have all, in their distinctive ways, approached the questions posed by the very fact of living in their world. Where did it come from? Who made it and why?

Today a modern voice is heard asking the same questions and giving his answer.

And God stepped out on space,
And he looked around and said:
I'm lonely—
I'll make me a world.

Then God sat down—
On the side of a hill where he could think,
By a deep river he sat down;
With his head in his hands,
God thought and thought,
Till he thought: I'll make me a man!

(James Weldon Johnson)

It is the same theme of Creation that dominates the group of stories called 'Creation myths' that come from the religious and cultural environment of the ancient Hebrew, as he began his account of Creation with the majestic 'In the beginning—'!

The Hebrew account, although showing evidence of awareness of the environment of other nations and cultures, neither slavishly copied nor took over wholesale such stories of their neighbours, but used such material to express their distinctive religious faith. The Israelite faith is unique. Old allusions such as to Rahab, Leviathan and the Dragon (see Ps. 74; Job 26; Isa. 27.51; Heb. 3. 9) have been taken from a context of many gods and a religion of natural processes, and made to serve as witness to Yahweh, Lord of all human history.

The biblical teaching concerning Creation may be summarised in the making of four affirmations.

Creation is a witness to Sovereignty

The very beginning is like a roll of drums:

In the beginning God created the heavens and the earth

(Gen. 1.1)

This is in direct contrast to any idea such as the later Greek idea of 'cosmos', a universe as a rationally constituted and self-sustaining structure of reality. The Bible account is not concerned to describe a theory about any process of what happened, but to make a declaration about God. If God is the Creator then he is to be worshipped because there is a personal relationship between the Creator and the Creation. The Hebrew doctrine of Creation is really a summons to worship the Sovereign Lord.

These are the notes that dominate such writings as the following illustrative passages.

The theme of the creative personal word is found in the repeated refrain of Gen. 1:

And God said, ' Let there be light '; and there was light.

The note is heard again in psalmist and prophet. So we read:

Let all the earth fear the Lord
let all the inhabitants of the world stand in awe of him!
For he spoke, and it came to be;
he commanded, and it stood forth!

(Ps. 33. 8–9; see also Ps. 148.5)

So, too, the prophet bears his witness to the Sovereign Lord whose creative word has gone forth:

I made the earth,
and created man upon it;
it was my hands that stretched out the heavens
and I commanded all their host (Isa. 45. 12)

For thus says the Lord,
who created the heavens (he is God!),
who formed the earth and made it (he established it; he did not create a chaos, he formed it to be inhabited!):
I am the Lord, and there is no other! (Isa. 45. 18)

Such passages clearly represent much more than speculation about the world's beginnings. They are a proclamation of Creation's King!

Creation because of Redemption

One of the striking features of the Hebrew records is that in the early creed there is a silence concerning God as Creator. So we read in one of the first of these formulations:

> And you shall make response before the Lord your God. A wandering Aramean was my father; and he went down into Egypt and sojourned there, few in number; and there he became a nation, great, mighty and populous . . . then we cried to the Lord the God of our fathers, and the Lord heard our voice, and saw our affliction, our toil, and our oppression; and the Lord brought us out of Egypt with a mighty hand. . . .
>
> (Deut. 26. 5–9; see also Josh. 24. 3–7)

Of course, no one suggests that the ancient Hebrew has got his thinking so mixed up that he thinks the Exodus was actually before the Creation. Yet the essential point is that only that God who brought his people out of Egypt, out of the house of bondage, could possibly be the Creator of the world! *The experience of having been delivered* is the source o the Hebrew certainty that there could be no other god, no alternative creator.

Especially in Second Isaiah do we find this integral link made between Redeemer and Creator. Creation and Redemption become interchangeable terms.

This is why God created the world: so that he might have a living context of persons to whom he could reveal his gracious redeeming purpose. In this sense, it is true to say that God is Redeemer before he is Creator.

> But now thus says the Lord,
> he who created you, O Jacob,
> he who formed you, O Israel:
> Fear not, for I have redeemed you;
> I have called you by name, you are mine
> When you pass through the waters I will be with you,
> and through rivers, they shall not overwhelm you;——
> For I am the Lord your God,
> the Holy One of Israel, your Saviour
> I gave Egypt as your ransom.
>
> (Isa. 43. 1–2; see also Isa. 48. 8–12)

In this passage the prophet can find no other way of describing the return from Babylon. The return from Exile is a Second Exodus—a new Creation.

Creation and Consummation

A further feature of the biblical view of Creation is that Creation is never thought of as an act that is completed at a single stroke, once for all. The created world is threatened and needs the constant sustaining power of God. He is no *deus ex machina*, nor can he stand in the wings of life's drama and just watch the world go by!

Two passages bring out essential emphases, that Creation is a continuing act of God and that Creation points forward to a completion. There is a Beginning that demands an Ending. In the beginning God—and at the End too! This may be seen in the prophet's words:

Thus says the Lord, the King of Israel and his Redeemer,
the Lord of hosts:
I am the first and I am the last;
besides me there is no god. (Isa. 44. 6)

Hearken to me, O Jacob,
and Israel, whom I called!
I am he, I am the first,
and I am the last. (Isa. 48. 12)

This affirmation must not be understood as a cycle that repeats itself (see Eccles. 1), but God will work out the purpose of Creation when the world he created will come to its consummation. In technical theological language, Creation points forward to an 'Eschatology' (Last Things)—the Beginning demands an Ending.

The continuing care of the Creator is illustrated by the psalmist:

These all look to thee,
to give them their food in due season.
When thou givest to them, they gather it up;
when thou openest thy hand, they are filled with good things.
When thou hidest thy face, they are dismayed;
when thou takest away their breath they die and return to the
dust.
When thou sendest forth thy Spirit, they are created;
and thou renewest the face of the ground.
(Ps. 104. 28–30; see also Pss. 97, 98, 100)

In another prophetic passage we find that in speaking of the creative power of God he uses a verbal form that stresses the permanent creative role of God:

Thus says the Lord, your Redeemer,
who formed you from the womb:

I am the Lord, who made all things,
who stretched out the heavens alone,
who spread out the earth by myself.

(Isa. 44.24)

The phrase 'who made all things' uses the present participle and a better translation would be 'who keeps on making all things'.

In the past, the present and the future, the Lord God remains the Creator.

The New Creation in Christ

The very core of the New Testament teaching is the affirmation that the New Creation has dawned in the coming of Christ. We hear this note again and again:

Therefore, if any one is in Christ, he is a new creation; the old has passed away, behold, the new has come.

(II Cor. 5. 17; see Rom. 5. 12–14)

For neither circumcision counts for anything, nor
    uncircumcision,
but a new creation.

(Gal. 6. 15; Ephes. 2. 10; Romans 6.4)

This theme continues throughout the Bible and in its closing pages we find the vision of Creation's purpose being fulfilled. A foretaste of this victory of God's creative purpose we see in such passages as the following:

Worthy art thou, our Lord and God,
to receive glory and honour and power,
for thou didst create all things,
and by thy will they existed and were created.

(Rev. 4. 11; 5. 13)

There is much more here than a backward look to the first Creation. The fuller creation through Christ, the renewal and climax of God's original purpose, is celebrated in the great picture of the New Jerusalem:

Then I saw a new heaven and a new earth; for the first heaven and the first earth had passed away and the sea was no more. And I saw the holy city, new Jerusalem coming down out of heaven from God, prepared as a bride adorned for her husband . . . . And he who sat upon the throne said: Behold, I make all things new.

(Rev. 21. 1, 2, 5)

67

The purpose of the Creator God has been realised through Christ and we are charged to bear witness to this fact through the power that comes along from our living relationship with a living Christ.

Behold, the dwelling of God is with me,
He will dwell with them, and they shall be his people,
and God himself shall be with them; he will wipe away
every tear from their eyes, and death shall be no more,
neither shall there be mourning nor crying nor pain any more
for the former things have passed away.

(Rev. 21. 3–4)

Here is the victory of God's purpose or Creation seen as present possession yet to be fulfilled in its fullest consummation. An acute comment has been made: 'The present period of the Church is the time between the decisive battle, which has already occurred, and the Victory Day'. (O. Cullman, *Christ and Time*, p. 145.)

RICHES: A Bible Study

At no time of the year, save perhaps Christmas, are we more conscious of our material wealth as a nation, more sensitive about the less fortunate. Dr Edgar Jones illuminates biblical teaching on wealth, poverty and true riches

We frequently are told that 'You can't take it with you!' By which slogan we are presented with a tabloid philosophy of wealth. While the verdict is unexceptionable, it still leaves unanswered the bare problem—what do we do with it here when we've got it?

In this brief study we seek to find the Bible guide-lines that are desperately needed in a world that is characterised as divided between the Haves—and the Have-nots.

We shall look in turn at the Old Testament, then the development of its teaching in the New Testament and, supremely, the difference that belief in the Lordship of Christ makes.

In the Old Testament we find soon a dominant emphasis, that is, the direct causal link between the prosperous and the good—the one because the other.

Riches and Righteousness
In a number of passages we find the direct link made between riches and righteousness. Prosperity is seen as a direct outcome and reward for a man's goodness and integrity.

I have been young, and now am old;
yet I have not seen the righteous forsaken or his children
    begging bread (Ps. 37. 25)

So, too, the causal connection is implicit in the tribute paid to Job in the Prologue of that work:

There were born to him seven sons and three daughters. He had seven thousand sheep, three thousand camels, five hundred yoke of oxen, and five hundred she-asses, and very many servants; so that this man was the greatest of all the people of the east. (Job 1.3)

This verdict is integrally connected with the character assessment of the opening verse:

There was a man in the land of Uz, whose name was Job; and that man was blameless and upright, one who feared God, and turned away from evil (v. 1).

It is because of his piety that he knew prosperity. So far all is for the best in the best possible world. The equation is automatic —be good and you'll prosper. To the righteous riches will come as night follows day.

The questioning of the axiom

The formula that belongs to the neat and tidy moral world where all is black and white does not satisfy the human mind for long, and the Old Testament itself provides the material for the criticism of, and ultimate rejection of, such easy superficial verdicts— prizes for the good and punishment for the evil.

In the following passages we note a greater realism.

Why do the wicked live, reach old age, and grow mighty in power? (Job 21. 7)

Woe to those who live upon beds of ivory,
and stretch themselves upon their couches,
and eat lambs from the flock,
and calves from the midst of the stall. (Amos 6. 4)

Hear this, you who trample upon the needy,
and bring the poor of the land to an end,
saying ' When will the new moon be over,
that we may sell grain?
And the sabbath, that we may offer wheat for sale,
that we may make the ephah small and the shekel great,
and deal deceitfully with false balances
that we may buy the poor for silver and the needy for a pair
of sandals, and sell the refuse of the wheat?'

(Amos 8. 4–6; see also Isa. 10. 3; Jer. 5. 27; Hos. 12. 8; Micah 6. 12)

The possession of riches is no longer taken as automatic evidence of God's favour. It can be the means of blessing, or the cause of his wrath.

Social realism concerning riches

The Wisdom writers have a greater social realism concerning wealth and the impact it makes upon human relationships.

Treasures gained by wickedness do not profit but righteousness delivers from death (Prov. 10. 2)

A rich man's wealth is his strong city; the poverty of the poor is their ruin. (10. 15)

Wealth brings many new friends but a poor man is deserted by his friends (19. 4)

The poor use entreaties but the rich answers roughly (18. 23)

Especially does the Preacher give his crushing verdict upon the acquisition of wealth for its own sake:

I made great works; I built houses and planted vineyards for myself; I made myself gardens and parks and planted in them all kinds of fruit trees—
I had also great possessions of herds and flocks, more than any who had been before me in Jerusalem (Ecclesiastes 2. 4–7)

Yet the final verdict is:

Behold all was vanity and a striving after wind, and there was nothing to be gained under the sun (2. 11)

The Old Testament thought concerning riches is not static. From seeing wealth and possessions as a mark of due favour, it advances to the realisation that they can become a stumbling-block and alienate a man from his fellows and his God. They can be a gift to enjoy but never a source of ultimate security. (See Prov. 11. 38; 8. 18; 27. 24; Eccles. 5. 15–16).

As we turn to New Testament thought concerning wealth and riches we can crystallise its essential emphases in a number of themes.

The property perspective is bankrupt

The classic passage in support of the first New Testament affirmation is the Beatitude:

Blessed are the poor in spirit for theirs is the kingdom of heaven (Matt. 5. 3)

Blessed are you poor, for yours is the kingdom of God (Luke 6. 20)

These verses do not mean that Jesus is taking sides in a political and economic struggle, and the additional comment of Matthew is designed to bring out the meaning of the Aramaic

71

phrase that is used for 'the poor'. It goes far beyond any income-bracket allocation. The 'poor' in Biblical thought, which figured largely in the Psalter, had come to represent the class of hard-working humble folk who looked to God for their redemption and trusted neither political structure nor material possessions for their ultimate security.

This is not to understand the New Testament as maintaining that riches are morally neutral and that having or not having possessions is irrelevant. In fact, the realism of the Old Testament is continued in the New and Jesus emphasises the danger of riches rather than their neutrality:

> How hard it will be for those who have riches to enter the Kingdom of God! (Mark 10. 23)

Ultimate trust in riches is practical atheism

Another major insight of the New Testament is the realisation that lies behind a number of well-known passages—that is, that a man may come to trust so completely in his possessions that he has denied the existence of God. This can only be called Practical Atheism and the picture of the Rich Fool is a classic example of such spiritual poverty:

The climax is the rich man's confident soliloquy which is shattered by the rebuke of God:

> 'Man, you have plenty of good things laid by, enough for many years: take life easy, eat, drink and enjoy yourself.' But God said to him, 'You fool, this very night you must surrender your life; you have made your money—who will get it now?'
> (*NEB*, Luke 12. 16–21; also story of Dives and Lazarus, 16. 25)

That is how it is with the man who amasses for himself and remains a pauper in the sight of God.

The essential NT teaching is that a man's *attitude* to his possessions is all-important. Can he sit loose to possessions and place his ultimate trust in God himself—the Giver more than the goods? Richness of spirit comes from a relationship not a carefully amassed hoard of things, however valuable in themselves:

> Sell your possessions, and give alms, provide yourself with purses that do not grow old, with a treasure in the heavens that does not fail, where no thief approaches and no moth destroys. For where your treasure is, there will your heart be also.
> (Luke 12. 33–34; see also Mark 10. 17–22; 17. 23–27)

Possessions and partiality

In the writings of the early Church we find constantly the mind of Christ portrayed when the Church dares to be true to its Master. Yet the dilemma is evident as again and again the temptation is there to deal with persons as having power and possessions and so to be marked out for preferential treatment. So we have the warning strongly and starkly uttered:

> For if a man with gold rings and in fine clothing comes into your assembly, and a poor man in shabby clothing also comes in, and you pay attention to the one who wears fine clothing and say, ' Have a seat here, please ', while you say to the poor man, ' Stand there ' or, ' Sit at my feet ', have you not made distinctions among yourselves, and become judges with evil thoughts?
>
> (James 2. 2–4; also Rev. 3. 17; 18. 17; 1 Tim. 6. 8–9, 17, 18)

At the other pole, the early Church affords us a picture of a community that has resolved the question of riches and possessions. So we read:

> Now the company of those who believed were of one heart and soul, and no one said that any of the things which he possessed was his own, but they had everything in common— there was not a needy person among them (Acts 4. 32–37)

It is superficial to see this as an early economic attempt at redistribution. The core of the story is that such sharing was the expression rather of rededication—the reaffirming of a spiritual relationship to their Lord and as a consequence to each other. Once the spiritual dynamic is lost the economics fall apart (see the end of the story in Acts 5. 1–11).

Possessions and the person of Christ

Finally, we come to the Bible's greatest insight concerning the spiritual issues that underlie having wealth and abundance of possessions—the answer lies in the attitude and actions of Christ himself:

> For you know the grace of our Lord Jesus Christ, that though he was rich, yet for your sake he became poor, so that by his poverty you might become rich. (II Cor. 8. 9; see also II Cor. 6. 10)

Christ is the living example of what it is to be ' rich toward God ' which he bore witness to, in his living and his dying.

Our closing passage crystallises all the teaching of the New Testament that a man's riches are to be measured by the reality of his renunciation of all that might hinder his service to God and his fellows:

Have this mind among yourselves, which you have in Christ Jesus who, though he was in the form of God, did not count equality with God a thing to be grasped, but emptied himself, taking the form of a servant, being born in the likeness of man —and became obedient unto death on a cross. Therefore God has highly exalted him and bestowed on him the name which is above every name—— (Phil. 2. 5–11)

Here is the only context within which riches are to be reckoned—the new world of the Resurrection faith.

THE JEWISH FESTIVAL OF TABERNACLES

Myer Domnitz describes a double feast which looks back to harvest— and which Christians may see as also being related to Advent and the next step in God's dealing with men

Nine days at the end of September constitute the harvest festival of Tabernacles, a very happy season in the Jewish calendar, with its climax, on the ninth day, of *Simchat Torah* (rejoicings in the teachings and law of Judaism).

This festival, with Passover and the Feast of the Giving of the Ten Commandments (for the latter, see *Together*, May 1975), makes up the three Pilgrim festivals, when ' every year shall thy males appear before the Lord thy God in the place which he shall choose ' (Deut. 16. 16). It is so called because of the divine ruling: ' Ye shall dwell in booths (Hebrew *succoth*, ' tabernacles ') seven days, so that your generations may know that I made the Children of Israel to dwell in booths, when I brought them out of the land of Egypt ' (Lev. 23. 42–43).

Practising Jewish families erect their tabernacles in their gardens or yards, have all their meals and spend much time there during the festival. Many synagogues have communal tabernacles for their members unable to construct their own. The portable walls of the tabernacle are covered with attractive hangings. The roof consists of branches of trees, from which hang tasty fruits and fragrant flowers, and through which we get a glimpse of the skies. In early tabernacles, olive and palm branches and myrtles were used in the structure of the roof, and also vines from which clustering grapes still hung.

Children love to help in decorating the tabernacle with attractive drawings and pictures which add to its colourful and picturesque appearance.

The tabernacle, because of its temporary character and the fragility of the roof, through which we gaze heavenwards, is a striking reminder that the Children of Israel were able to dwell safely in their tabernacles in the wilderness only because of divine protection; and of God's providence and presence. There is also a strong link between the Jewish faith and the kindly manifestations of Nature in the observance of this and the other Pilgrim Festivals.

The following verses from the moving prayer recited in the tabernacle, on the first night of the festival, are illuminating: ' May it be thy will, O Lord my God and the God of my fathers, to let thy divine presence abide among us. Spread over us the tabernacle of thy peace in recognition of the precept of the tabernacle, which we are now fulfilling. Surround us with the pure and holy radiance of thy glory, that is spread over our heads as the eagle over the nest he stirs up; and thence bid the stream of life flow in upon thy servants. Blessed be the Lord for ever. Amen.'

The festival also has the picturesque name of ' the Feast of Ingathering ', as the people rejoiced because their heavenly Father blessed them with the fresh produce of field and garden. Linked with this is the biblical ruling: ' And you shall take unto you on the first day of the festival the fruit of the goodly tree, branches of palm trees and boughs of thick-leaved trees and willows of the brooks, and you shall rejoice before the Lord your God seven days ' (Lev. 23. 40). These branches are used in the synagogue in the recital of the Hallel (Hebrew hymns of praise, Psalms 113 to 118) in the festival morning service, as follows: a palm branch, to which is attached by palm leaves a flowering myrtle and willow, is held in the right hand and a citron (Hebrew *ethrog*) in the left. Among interesting interpretations of the use of these products of Nature are: the citron is a symbol of the heart, the palm of the spinal cord, the myrtle of the eye and the willow of the human lips. The purpose is to teach us that we must serve God with all our being. The four plants thus joined together are a witness of people *living together in harmony in God's presence*— colourfully given by the waving of the plants in all directions during the service.

The crowded procession of the bearers of the four plants— men of all ages—is a moving sight in the synagogue, which is reminiscent of the Temple ceremony when willow branches were placed on the altar and priests marched round it carrying palm branches and singing festival hymns. *Hoshaana Rabba* (Hebrew, ' the great *hoshaana* ') is the name of the seventh day of the festival, as on that day many prayers for salvation beginning with the word *hoshaana* (meaning ' save, we beseech thee ' and more familiar to Anglicans as ' hosanna! ') are recited during morning service. This day is connected with the Ten Days of Penitence, including the New Year and the Day of Atonement (see *Together*, August 1975); the devout are occupied the previous night in prayer and the study of holy works.

The following day, ' The Eighth Day of Solemn Assembly ', has in the Additional Service an impressive prayer composed in the eighth century, which is connected with the prayer recited by the people in ancient Israel for rain and fruitful harvests. This prayer has an enduring significance in drought areas. It asks for the coming of the vital rain, which will bring abundance and thus avoid famine; it is for life and not for death. From this day until the first day of the following Passover there is inserted in the daily prayers the phrase ' Thou causest the wind to blow and the rain to fall.' In the Holy Land this is the season when the rain falls.

This prayer also has links with the magnificent Temple ceremony of ' Drawing the Water ' in the Court of the Women during the night, when golden lamps lit up the joyful scene. The Levites stood on the fifteen steps between the Courts of the Women and of the Israelites, played their instruments and led the chanting of Psalms 120 to 134—' Songs of degrees ' as they are called, probably a reference to the steps on which the singers stood. The assembled people rejoiced before the Lord and the priests blessed them. Then the Levites recited from Psalm 128: ' May the Lord bless you out of Zion, may you see the good of Jerusalem all the days of your life.'

Then comes the final day of the festival, *Simchat Torah*. On every Sabbath throughout the year a portion of the Pentateuch (the Five Books of Moses) is read aloud in the synagogue from the sacred Hebrew scrolls in the Ark. On this joyous day, which begins on the previous evening with services, the public reading of the Pentateuch is completed with the last section of Deuteronomy, and a member of the congregation is honoured by being called to this reading as ' the bridegroom of the Law '. This is followed by the reading from the first section of Genesis, and the member called for this reading is honoured as ' the bridegroom of the first section of the Law '.

This is particularly a happy and purposeful day for the children, the growing generation, who learn from its ceremonies the remarkable continuity of the Torah in the life of the Jewish people throughout the world. They join in the processions of the sacred

77

scrolls around the synagogue, carrying decorative banners and brightly-lit candles, as all sing the cheerful hymns of Simchat Torah. Even the very young are on this day called to the reading from the sacred scrolls.

The spirit of this popular and heart-moving religious occasion is indicated in the following extract from a prayer for this festive day:

' This Feast of Law all your gladness display;
Today all your homages render;
My God I will promise in a jubilant lay;
My hope in him never surrender.
Then exult in the Law on its festive day—
The Law is our Light and Defender;
While my breath is, my lips all thy wonders shall say,
Thy truth and thy kindness so tender.'

Simchat Torah thus remains a remarkable witness that for thousands of years Jews have never ceased to read the Hebrew Bible and to study its commentaries and outstanding teachings which have developed from it through the generations. For the Torah of God, as this annual day of truly joyous remembrance and continuity makes clear, is ' a tree of life to them that grasp it ' (Proverbs 3. 18).

The following are sections from the Pentateuch which are read in the synagogue during the festival: Leviticus 22. 26 to 23. 44; Exodus 33. 12 to 34. 26; Deuteronomy 14. 22 to 16. 7 and on the final day Deuteronomy 33 to end of Pentateuch, and Genesis 1. 1 to 2. 3.

From the prophets and other biblical works the readings are from: Zechariah 14; I Kings 8. 2–21; Ezekiel 38. 18 to 39. 16; I Kings 7. 22–66; Joshua 1 and Ecclesiastes.